Contents

Glitzy Wrap 2

Delicate Web Wrap 6

Double-Up Wrap 10

Sherbet Triangle Wrap 12

Devon Cross Shawl 16

Pineapple Shells Capelet 20

Butterfly Garden Two-Way Shawl 24

Popcorns and Lace Shawl 28

Abbreviations and Stitch Symbols 31

Glitzy Wrap

Multi-fiber yarns are spun together from fibers of a variety of textures and colors. The yarn in this shoulder wrap blends warm mohair with shiny fibers for some glamour. Pull it around your shoulders in the evening while you're watching a movie! The pattern is worked from a center foundation row in both directions, so the lacy shells all face outward and create scallops at both narrow ends.

YARN
Bulky-weight multi-fiber yarn, approximately 800 yd (740m)

HOOK
10½/K (6.5 mm)

STITCHES USED
Single crochet

Double crochet

Triple crochet

GAUGE
1 shell cluster = 2¾" (7 cm)

NOTION
Tapestry needle

FINISHED SIZE
20" x 68" (51 x 173 cm)

Lacy open-work pattern of triple crochet shells.

FIRST HALF OF WRAP

Wrap is worked in 2 halves, both starting from same center ch.

Foundation row: Ch 57. Sc in second ch from hook, sk 3 ch, * work [tr, ch 2] 4 times in next ch, 1 more tr in same ch (shell CL made), sk 3 ch, sc in next ch, rep from * 6 times more (7 shell CL), turn.

Row 1: Ch 5 (counts as 1 tr, ch 2), work 1 dc in the first ch-2 sp, * ch 3, sk next ch-2 sp, 1 sc in top of third tr of shell CL, ch 3, sk next ch-2 sp, 1 dc in next ch-2 sp, ch 2, 1 dc in next ch-2 sp, rep from * 5 times more, end ch 3, 1 sc in third tr of shell CL, ch 3, sk next ch-2 sp, 1 dc in next ch-2 sp, ch 2, 1 tr in last sc, turn.

Row 2: Ch 5 (counts as 1 tr, ch 2), work [1 tr, ch 2, 1 tr] in first tr (half shell CL made), * 1 sc in next sc, [1 tr, ch 2] 4 times in next ch-2 sp, 1 more tr in same sp, rep from * 5 times more, end 1 sc in next sc, [1 tr, ch 2, 1 tr, ch 2, 1 tr] all in third ch of tch (half shell CL made) (half shell CL at beg of row, 6 full shell CL, half shell CL at end of row), turn.

Row 3: Ch 1, work 1 sc in first tr, ch 3, 1 dc in second ch-2 sp, * ch 2, 1 dc in next ch-2 sp, ch 3, 1 sc in third tr of CL, ch 3, sk 1 ch-2 sp, 1 dc in next ch-2 sp, rep from * 5 times more, end 1 dc in next ch-2 sp, ch 3, 1 sc in third ch of tch, turn.

Each end of wrap is scalloped because wrap is worked from center out in both directions.

Row 4: Ch 1, work 1 sc in first sc, * [tr, ch 2] 4 times in next ch-2 sp, 1 more tr in same sp, 1 sc in next sc, rep from * 6 times more (7 shell CL), turn.

Rep rows 1 through 4 for 34" (86.5 cm), ending with row 4, fasten off.

SECOND HALF OF WRAP

Join yarn in right corner of beg ch. Working on other side of ch, rep patt beg at foundation row, fasten off.

FINISHING

Weave in ends using tapestry needle.

Delicate Web Wrap

Spider web—the small, alternating shell pattern in this shoulder wrap—looks like vintage lace. Made of lightweight microfiber yarn, the wrap is not only ultrasoft and feminine, but also warm.

YARN
Lightweight microfiber yarn, approximately 1,340 yd (1,233 m)

HOOK
8/H (5 mm)

STITCHES USED
Single crochet

Double crochet

GAUGE
4 shell clusters = 4" (10 cm)

NOTION
Tapestry needle

FINISHED SIZE
25" x 60" (63.5 x 152.5 cm)

Staggered placement of shell clusters results in a delicate, lacy web of stitches.

WRAP

Wrap is worked in 1 piece.

To create the staggered placement of shells from row to row, odd rows beg and end with a half CL, even rows beg and end with a full CL.

Foundation row: Ch 110. Starting in second ch from hook, work 1 sc, * sk 2 ch, [1 dc, ch 1, 1 dc, ch 1, 1 dc] in next ch (shell CL made), sk 2 ch, 1 sc in next ch, rep from * across, end 1 sc in last ch (18 shell CL).

Row 1: Ch 4 (counts as 1 dc, ch 1), work 1 dc in first sc, sk 1 dc, 1 sc in next dc (center of shell), sk next dc, *[1 dc, ch 1, 1 dc, ch 1, 1 dc] in next sc, sk 1 dc, 1 sc in next sc, sk next dc, rep from * across, end [1 dc, ch 1, 1 dc] in last st (17 full shell CL and a half shell on each end), turn.

Scalloped shell border perfectly finishes the edges of the wrap.

Row 2: Ch 1, work 1 sc in first dc, * [1 dc, ch 1, 1 dc, ch 1, 1 dc] in next sc, sk 1 dc, 1 sc in next dc, rep from * across, end sk 1 dc, [1 dc, ch 1, 1 dc, ch 1, 1 dc] in next sc, 1 sc in next dc, 1 sc in third ch of tch (18 full shell CL), turn.

Rep rows 1 and 2 until wrap is 58" (147 cm) long, do not fasten off.

BORDER

With right side facing you, ch 3, work 2 dc in same st (this is half of the first corner). Working along long edge of wrap, * work [3 dc, ch 2, 3 dc] in next sp (created by turning chains), 1 sc in next sp, rep from * to bottom, [3 dc, ch 2, 3 dc] in last st (second corner), rep from * working along foundation ch to last st, work corner in last st, cont up other long edge, work corner in last st, cont along top edge, ending with 3 dc in same st as beg, join with Sl st to form last corner.

FINISHING

Weave in ends using tapestry needle.

Double-Up Wrap

This shoulder wrap is made by crocheting together two yarns of totally different textures using an extra-large hook. One yarn has mohair and other fibers that make the wrap warm and fuzzy. The other yarn is a smooth, shiny ladder yarn. This wrap can be finished fast, and the result is stunning.

WRAP

Wrap is worked in 1 piece, with 1 strand of each yarn held tog throughout.

Foundation row: Ch 23 loosely. Starting in second ch from hook, work 1 sc in each ch across (22 sc), turn.

Row 1: Ch 1 (counts as a sc), sk first st, work 1 sc in each st across, 1 sc in tch, turn.

Rep row 1 until piece measures 52" (132 cm), fasten off.

FINISHING

Weave in ends using tapestry needle.

FRINGE

Wrap both yarns around 8" (20.5 cm) piece of cardboard 44 times. Cut yarn at bottom to make 44 double strands, each 16" (40.5 cm) long. Fold a double strand in half and, using a crochet hook, pull lp through first st at one narrow end of wrap. Put tails of double strand through lp and pull tails to snug lp up to edge of wrap. Rep at each st across both ends of wrap.

YARN
Bulky-weight multi-fiber yarn

Bulky-weight ribbon yarn, approximately 410 yd (380 m) of each

HOOK
P/Q (15 mm)

STITCH USED
Single crochet

GAUGE
6 sc = 4" (10 cm)

NOTIONS
Tapestry needle

8" (20.5 cm) piece of cardboard

FINISHED SIZE
15" x 52" (38 x 132 cm) not including fringe

Ladder yarn and multi-fiber yarn held together and worked in single crochet with a large hook.

Sherbet Triangle Wrap

To create this unusual shoulder wrap, you start at the point and work toward the top. The yarn is dyed in a rainbow of colors that change as you hook along. The crosshatch stitch pattern is fun to work as you watch the colors develop into a complex and very beautiful surface.

YARN

Lightweight smooth yarn for throw,

Medium-weight ribbon yarn, approximately 550 yd (506 m) for fringe, approximately 220 yd (202 m)

HOOK

9/I (5.5 mm)

STITCH USED

Double crochet

GAUGE

5 clusters = 4" (10 cm)

(1 cluster = ch 3, 3 dc in same ch lp)

NOTIONS

Tapestry needle

9" (23 cm) piece of cardboard

FINISHED SIZE

52" x 24" (132 x 61 cm), not including fringe

Lightweight rayon/metallic yarn worked in double crochet clusters.

WRAP

Wrap is worked in 1 piece from lower point to long upper edge.

Row 1: Ch 5 (counts as a dc, called ch lp now and throughout), work 3 dc into fifth ch from hook (1 CL made, 4 sts total), turn.

Row 2: Ch 5, work 3 dc into fifth ch from hook, Sl st into ch lp of next CL, ch 3, work 3 dc into same ch lp (2 CL made), turn.

Row 3: Ch 5, work 3 dc into fifth ch from hook, Sl st into ch lp of next CL, ch 3, work 3 dc into same ch lp, Sl st into ch lp of next CL, ch 3, work 3 dc into same ch lp (3 CL made), turn.

Row 4: Ch 5, work 3 dc into fifth ch from hook, Sl st into ch lp of next CL, ch 3, work 3 dc into same ch lp, Sl st into ch lp of next CL, ch 3, work 3 dc into same ch lp, Sl st into ch lp of next CL, ch 3, work 3 dc into same ch lp (4 CL made).

Cont to work in this manner, beg every row with ch 5, 3 dc into fifth ch from hook, CL in each ch lp across row, ending with CL in last ch lp. You will have 1 more CL at the end of each row. Work until the entire ball of yarn is used (about 50 rows).

Last row of clusters at upper edge forms dainty scallops.

FINISHING

Weave in ends using tapestry needle.

FRINGE

Wrap ribbon yarn around 9" (23 cm) piece of cardboard about 300 times. Cut yarn at bottom to make 300 strands, each 18" (46 cm) long. Fold 2 strands in half and, using a crochet hook, pull lp through st at lower point of wrap. Put tails of double strand through lp, and pull tails to snug lp up to edge of wrap. Rep along both diagonal sides of wrap, evenly spacing about 75 fringes on each side.

Devon Cross Shawl

Stitching lacy granny squares is a fun way to create spectacular projects. This shawl was created by crocheting and joining Devon Cross grannies in a way that results in a very lacy, lightweight, and luxurious wrap.

SHAWL

Make 20 Devon Cross Squares (page 19); assemble squares as follows:

Working on any square, with WS facing:

Row 1: Sc in corner sp, *[ch 5, skip next 2 dc, sc in next dc] 4 times, ch 5, sc in next sc, ch 5, sc in next dc, [ch 5, skip next 2 dc, sc in next dc] 3 times, ch 5, sc in last corner sp on this side of square*, place second square along side of square just worked, ch 5, sc in corner sp of new square, rep from * to *, ch 3, (you will now have worked along one end of two squares), turn work 180 degrees so work just **completed is upside down.**

Row 2: (join 2 more squares as follows): Sc in corner sp of new square, * [ch 2, sl st in center ch of previous ch-5 sp, ch 2, skip next 2 dc, sc in next dc] 4 times, ch 2, sl st in center ch of previous ch-5 sp, ch 2, sc in next sc, ch 2, sl st in center ch of previous ch-5 sp, ch 2, sc in next dc, [ch 2, sl st in center ch of previous ch-5 sp, ch 2, skip next 2 dc, sc in next dc] 3 times, ch 2, sl st in center ch of previous ch-5 sp, ch 2, sc in corner sp*, ch 2, sl st in center ch of previous ch-5 sp, ch 2, sc in corner of new square, rep from * to *, ch 3, sl st in sc from Row 1, (you will now have 4 squares joined), fasten off.

Rep Rows 1 and 2 until 12 squares are joined, turn, so that long, unworked area is ready to be joined. Rep Row 1 again, working all center joins between four squares with [ch 2, sl st] in same join as previously worked, ch 2, continue to end, ch 3, turn. Rep Row 2 to end.

Rep from beginning, with remaining 8 squares to form V shape.

(continued)

YARN
Lace weight, approximately 1,160 yd (1,067 m)

HOOK
F/5 (3.75 mm)

GAUGE
1 square = 6 × 6" (15 × 15 cm)

FINISHED SIZE
18 × 52" (45 × 132 cm)

EDGING

With RS facing and starting at bottom inside corner of short edge, attach yarn with sl st to center ch.

Row 1: 2 sc in corner sp, *sc in each of next 12 dc, 2 sc in ch-2 sp, sc in next sc, 2 sc in next ch-2 sp, sc in each of next 12 dc, 2 sc in corner sp,** sc in next sc, 3 sc in ch-3 sp, sc in next sc, 2 sc in ch-3 sp. Rep from * to end of side corner, 3 sc in corner sp. Rep from * around to last corner before V-shape of neck, sc in corner, skip side of next sc, sc in V-corner, skip side of next sc. Rep from *, ending at **, join with sl st to beg sc, do not turn.

Row 2: Ch 4 (counts as dc, ch 1), *skip next sc, [dc in next sc, ch 1, skip next sc] to next turning corner sp, [dc, ch 3, dc, ch 1] in center sc of corner. Rep from * to end with last dc in center sc of corner, turn.

Row 3: Ch 3 (counts as dc), [dc in next dc, dc in next sp] 2 times, dc in next dc, *ch 5, skip next 2 ch-1 sps, tr in next sp, ch 5, skip next 2 dc, [dc in next dc, dc in next sp] 3 times, dc in next dc. Rep from * to last 4 dc before turning corner sp, (dc in next dc, dc in next sp) 3 times, dc in next dc, ch 5, tr in center sp of corner, ch 5, (dc in next dc, dc in next sp) 3 times, dc in next dc.** Rep from * to last 3 dc before next turning corner, (dc in next dc, dc in next sp) 2 times, dc in next dc, ch 5, tr in center sp of corner, ch 5, [dc in next dc, dc in next sp] 2 times, dc in next dc. Rep from * to ** one time, then rep from * again to last 3 dc, [dc in next dc, dc in next sp] 2 times, dc in 3rd ch of turning ch, turn.

Row 4: Ch 3 (counts as dc), dc in each of next 3 dc, ch 7, sc in next tr, ch 7, *skip next dc, dc in each of next 5 dc, ch 7, sc in next tr, ch 7. Rep from * to 5-dc group before bottom corner, [dc in each of next 5 dc, ch 7, sc in next tr, ch 7] 2 times. Rep from * to last 5-dc group, skip next dc, dc in each of last 4 dc, turn.

Row 5: Ch 3 (counts as dc), dc in each of next 2 dc, *ch 7, (sc, ch 5, sc) in next sc, ch 7, skip next dc, dc in each of next 3 dc. Rep from * across, with last dc in top of turning ch, turn.

Row 6: Ch 6 (counts as dc, ch 3), *[dtr2tog, ch 3] 5 times in next ch-5 sp, skip next dc, dc in next dc, ch 3. Rep from * to next corner, ch 5, [(dtr2tog, ch 3) 4 times, dtr2tog] in next ch-5 sp, ch 5, skip next dc, dc in next dc, ch 3**. Rep from * to ** two more times, rep from * to end, with last dc in top of turning ch, turn.

Row 7: Sl st in first ch-3 sp, ch 1, sc in same sp, *[(ch 5, sc) in each of next 5 sps**, sc in next sp] repeat from * to next corner, ch 6, [sc, ch 5] in each of next 3 sps, sc in next sp, ch 6, sc in each of next 2 sps. Rep from * across, ending last rep at **, sl st in top of turning ch. Fasten off.

FINISHING

Blocking: Lay shawl on a padded surface, sprinkle with water, pat in shape, and allow to dry.

DEVON CROSS SQUARE

Ch 6, join with a Sl st to form a ring.

Rnd 1: Ch 3 (counts as dc here and throughout), 4 dc in ring, ch 8 [5 dc, ch 8] 3 times in ring, join with a Sl st in 3rd ch of beg ch-3 (4 ch-8 sps).

Rnd 2: Sl st in next 4 dc and in next ch-8 sp, ch 3, (2 dc, ch 3, 3 dc) in same sp, ch 5, *(3 dc, ch 3, 3 dc) in next ch-8 sp, ch 5, rep from * twice, join with Sl st in 3rd ch of beg ch-3.

Rnd 3: Ch 3, 1 dc in each of next 2 dc, *(3 dc, ch 3, 3 dc) in next ch-3 sp, 1 dc in each of next 3 dc, ch 2, 1 sc in center ch of next ch-5 sp, ch 2**, 1 dc in each of next 3 dc, rep from * twice, rep from * to ** once, join with a Sl st in 3rd ch of beg ch-3.

Rnd 4: Ch 3, 1 dc in each of next 5 dc, *(3 dc, ch 3, 3 dc) in next ch-3 sp, 1 dc in each of next 6 dc, ch 5, sk next 2 ch-2 sps**, 1 dc in each of next 6 dc, rep from * twice, rep from * to ** once, join with a Sl st in 3rd ch of beg ch-3.

Rnd 5: Ch 3, 1 dc in each of next 8 dc, *(3 dc, ch 3, 3 dc) in next ch-3 sp, 1 dc in each of next 9 dc, ch 2, 1 sc in 3rd ch of next ch-5 sp, ch 2**, 1 dc in each of next 9 dc, rep from * twice, rep from * to ** once, join with a Sl st in 3rd ch of beg ch-3.

Rnd 6: Ch 1, starting in same st, *1 sc in each of next 12 dc, (2 sc, ch 3, 2 sc) in next ch-3 sp, 1 sc in each of next 12 dc, 2 sc in next ch-2 sp, 1 sc in next sc, 2 sc in next ch-2 sp, rep from * around, join with a Sl st in first sc. Fasten off.

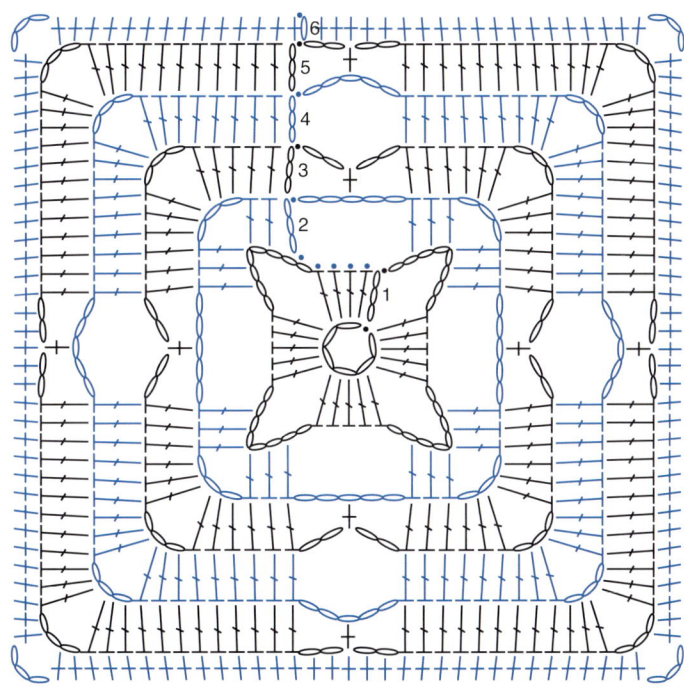

Pineapples and Shells Capelet

Grab a needle and silky mohair yarn to crochet a fashionable wrap that features an appealing drape. Because this lacy shell stitch makes increasing easy, you will want to create capelets that match every one of your dressy outfits.

Skill Level: Experienced

Notes: Triple crochet 3 together (tr3tog): [yo hook 2 times, pick up loop in designated stitch, (yo hook, pull through 2 lps) 2 times] 3 times, yo, pull through all 4 loops on hook.

This garment is worked in the round from top to bottom. Do not turn at the end of a round.

BEGIN

Using F/5 (3.75) hook ch 165, join with sl st to first ch to form a ring.

Foundation Rnd: Ch 3, 1 dc in same st as joining (counts as half shell), *ch 4, skip 6 chs, [1 dc, ch 4, 1 dc] in next ch, ch 4, skip 6 chs, [2 dc, ch 2, 2 dc] in next ch, rep from * around, end 2 dc in same ch as beg ch-3, ch 2, join with sl st to 3rd ch of beg ch-3 (this completes shell).

Rnd 1: Ch 3, work 1 dc slightly behind beg ch-3 in the ch-2 sp (half shell made), * ch 2, skip (ch-4 and 1 dc), in next ch-4 sp work [(tr3tog, ch 3) 3 times, tr3tog] ch 2, skip (1 dc, the ch-4, and 2 dc), [2 dc, ch 2, 2 dc] in next ch-2 sp, rep from * around, end 2 dc in last ch-2 sp, ch 2, join with sl st to 3rd ch of beg ch-3.

Rnd 2: Ch 3, work 1 dc slightly behind beg ch-3 (half shell made), * ch 3, skip (ch-2 sp and first tr3tog), [2 sc in next ch-3 sp, ch 3] 3 times, ch 2, skip (tr3tog, ch-2 and 2 dc), [2 dc, ch 2, 2 dc] in next ch-2 sp, rep from * around, end 2 dc in last ch-2 sp, ch 2, join with sl st to 3rd ch of beg ch-3.

Rnd 3: Ch 3, work 1 dc slightly behind beg ch-3 in ch-2 sp (half shell made), * ch 4, skip (ch-3 and 2 sc), 2 sc in next ch-3 sp, ch 3, 2 sc in next ch-3 sp, ch 4, skip (ch-3 and 2 dc), [2 dc, ch 2, 2 dc] in next ch-2 sp, rep from * around, end 2 dc in last ch-2 sp, ch 2, join with sl st to 3rd ch of beg ch-3.

(continued)

YARN
Lightweight silk/mohair blend approximately 400 yds (366 m)

HOOKS
F/5 (3.75 mm)
G/6 (4.00 mm)

GAUGE
With F/5 (3.75 mm) hook, 1 Pineapple group and 1 shell = 3" (7.6 cm)

FINISHED SIZE
12" long (30.4 cm), 56" (142.2 cm) wide at bottom

"Love Letter" fascinator by Ashliegh in Wonderland

Rnd 4: Ch 3, work 1 dc slightly behind beg ch-3 in ch-2 sp * ch 4, skip (2 dc, ch-4 and 2 sc), [1 dc, ch 4, 1 dc] in next ch-3 sp, ch 4, skip (ch-4 and 2 dc), [2 dc, ch 2, 2 dc] in next ch-2 sp, rep from * around, end 2 dc in last ch-2 sp, ch 2, join with sl st to 3rd ch of beg ch-3.

Rnd 5: Ch 3, work 1 dc slightly behind beg ch-3 in ch-2 sp (half shell made), * ch 3, skip (ch-4 and 1 dc), in next ch-4 sp work [(tr3tog, ch 3) 3 times, tr3tog] ch 3, skip (1 dc, ch-4, and 2 dc), [2 dc, ch 2, 2 dc] in next ch-2 sp, rep from * around, end 2 dc in last ch-2 sp, ch 2, join with sl st to 3rd ch of beg ch-3.

Rnd 6: Ch 3, work 1 dc slightly behind beg ch-3 (half shell made), * ch 4, skip (ch-3 sp and first tr3tog), [2 sc in next ch-3 sp, ch 3] 3 times, ch 4, skip tr3tog, skip (ch-3 and 2 dc), [2 dc, ch 2, 2 dc] in next ch-2 sp, rep from * around, end 2 dc in last ch-2 sp, ch 2, join with sl st to 3rd ch of beg ch-3.

Rnd 7: Ch 3, work 1 dc slightly behind beg ch-3 in ch-2 sp (half shell made), * ch 5, skip (ch-4 and 2 sc), 2 sc in next ch-3 sp, ch 3, 2 sc in next ch-3 sp, ch 5, skip (ch-4 and 2 dc) [2 dc, ch 2, 2 dc] in next ch-2 sp, rep from * around, end 2 dc in last ch-2 sp, ch 2, join with sl st to 3rd ch of beg ch-3.

Rnd 8: Ch 3, work 1 dc slightly behind beg ch-3 in ch-2 sp * ch 5, skip (2 dc, ch-5 and 2 sc), [1 dc, ch 4, 1 dc] in next ch-3 sp, ch 5, skip (ch 5 and 2 dc), [2 dc, ch 2, 2 dc] in next ch-2 sp, rep from * around, end 2 dc in last ch-2 sp, ch 2, join with sl st to 3rd ch of beg ch-3.

Change to G/6 (4.00 mm) hook.

Rnd 9: Ch 3, work 1 dc slightly behind beg ch-3 in ch-2 sp (half shell made), * ch 3, skip (ch-5 and 1 dc), in next ch-4 sp work [(tr3tog, ch 3) 3 times, tr3tog], ch 3, skip (1 dc, ch-5, and 2 dc), [2 dc, ch 2, 2 dc] in next ch-2 sp, rep from * around, end 2 dc in last ch-2 sp, ch 2, join with sl st to 3rd ch of beg ch-3.

Rnd 10: Ch 3, work 2 dc slightly behind beg ch-3 in ch-2 sp (half shell made), * ch 4, skip (ch-3 sp and first tr3tog), 2 sc in next ch-3 sp, [ch 3, 2 sc in next ch-3 sp] 2 times, ch 4, skip tr3tog, skip (ch-3 and 2 dc), [3 dc, ch 2, 3 dc] in next ch-2 sp, rep from * around, end 3 dc in last ch-2 sp, ch 2, join with sl st to 3rd ch of beg ch-3.

Rnd 11: Ch 3, work 2 dc slightly behind beg ch-3 in ch-2 sp (half shell made), *ch 5, skip (ch-4 and 2 sc), 2 sc in next ch-3 sp, ch 3, 2 sc in next ch-3 sp, ch 5, skip (ch-4 and 2 dc), [3 dc, ch 2, 3 dc] in next ch-2 sp, rep from * around, end 3 dc in last ch-2 sp, ch 2, join with sl st to 3rd ch of beg ch-3.

Rnd 12: Ch 3, work 2 dc slightly behind beg ch-3 in ch-2 sp (half shell made), * ch 5, skip (3 dc, ch-5 and 2 sc), [1 dc, ch 4, 1 dc] in next ch-3 sp, ch 5, skip (ch-5 and 3 dc), [3 dc, ch 2, 3 dc] in next ch-2 sp, rep from * around, end 3 dc in last ch-2 sp, ch 2, join with sl st to 3rd ch of beg ch-3.

Rnd 13: Ch 3, work 2 dc slightly behind beg ch-3 in ch-2 sp (half shell made), *ch 4, skip ch-5, in next ch-4 sp work [(tr3tog, ch 3) 3 times, tr3tog] ch 4, skip (ch-4, and 3 dc), [3 dc, ch 2, 3 dc] in next ch-2 sp, rep from * around, end 3 dc in last ch-2 sp, ch 2, join with sl st to 3rd ch of beg ch-3.

Rnd 14: Ch 3, work 2 dc slightly behind beg ch-3 (half shell made), * ch 6, skip (ch-4 and first tr3tog), 2 sc in next ch-3 sp, [ch 3, 2 sc in next ch-3 sp] 2 times, ch 6, skip tr3tog, skip (ch-3 and 2 dc), [3 dc, ch 2, 3 dc] in next ch-2 sp, rep from * around, end 3 dc in last ch-2 sp, ch 2, join with sl st to 3rd ch of beg ch-3.

Rnd 15: Ch 3, work 2 dc slightly behind beg ch-3 in ch-2 sp (half shell made), *ch 6, skip (ch-6 and 2 sc), 2 sc in next ch-3 sp, ch 3, 2 sc in next ch-3 sp, ch 6, skip (ch-6 and 3 dc), [3 dc, ch 2, 3 dc] in next ch-2 sp, rep from * around, end 3 dc in last ch-2 sp, ch 2, join with sl st to 3rd ch of beg ch-3.

Rnd 16: Ch 3, work 2 dc slightly behind beg ch-3 in ch-2 sp (half shell made) * ch 6, skip (3 dc, ch-6 and 2 sc), [1 dc, ch 4, 1 dc] in next ch-3 sp, ch 6, skip (ch-6 and 3 dc), [3 dc, ch 2, 3 dc] in next ch-2 sp, rep from * around, end 3 dc in last ch-2 sp, ch 2, join with sl st to 3rd ch of beg ch-3.

Rnd 17: Ch 3, work 2 dc slightly behind beg ch-3 in ch-2 sp (half shell made), * ch 4, skip (ch-6 and 1 dc), in next ch-4 sp work [(tr3tog, ch 3) 3 times, tr3tog] ch 6, skip (1 dc, ch-6, and 3 dc), [3 dc, ch 2, 3 dc] in next ch-2 sp, rep from * around, end 3 dc in last ch-2 sp, ch 2, join with sl st to 3rd ch of beg ch-3.

Rnd 18: Ch 3, work 2 dc slightly behind beg ch-3 in ch-2 sp (half shell made), * ch 4, skip (ch-4 sp and first tr3tog), 2 sc in next ch-3 sp, [ch 3, 2 sc in next ch-3 sp] 2 times, ch 4, skip tr3tog, skip (ch-4 and 3 dc), [3 dc, ch 2, 3 dc] in next ch-2 sp, rep from * around, end 3 dc in last ch-2 sp, ch 2, join with sl st to 3rd ch of beg ch-3.

Rnd 19: Ch 3, work 2 dc slightly behind beg ch-3 in ch-2 sp (half shell made), * ch 6, skip (ch-4 and 2 sc), 2 sc in next ch-3 sp, ch 3, 2 sc in next ch-3 sp, ch 6, skip (ch-4 and 3 dc), [3 dc, ch 4, 3 dc] in next ch-2 sp, rep from * around, end 3 dc in last ch-2 sp, ch 4, join with sl st to 3rd ch of beg ch-3.

Rnd 20: Ch 3, work 2 dc slightly behind beg ch-3 in ch-2 sp (half shell made), * ch 6, skip (3 dc, ch-4 and 2 sc), [1 dc, ch 4, 1 dc] in next ch-3 sp, ch 6, skip (ch-4 and 3 dc), [3 dc, ch 4, 3 dc] in next ch-2 sp, rep from * around, end 3 dc in last ch-2 sp, ch 2, join with sl st to 3rd ch of beg ch-3.

BOTTOM BORDER

Ch 9, skip ch-6, *work [(tr3tog, ch 3) 3 times, tr3tog] in next ch-4 sp, ch 6, skip next (ch-6 and 3 dc), rep from * around, end sl st to 3rd ch of beg ch-9. Fasten off.

NECK BORDER

With F/5 (3.75 mm) hook, join yarn at neck edge by joining.

Rnd 1: Ch 1, 6 sc in each sp created by 6 skipped chs, join with sl st to beg ch-1.

Rnd 2: Ch 5, (counts as 1 dc, ch-2) *skip 2 sc, 1 dc in next sc, rep from * around, end ch 2, sl st to 3rd ch of beg ch-5.

Rnd 3: Ch 1, *3 sc in next ch-2 sp, rep from * around, join with sl st to beg ch-1. Fasten off.

FINISHING

Blocking: Place on a padded surface, sprinkle with water, pat in shape, and pin. Let dry.

Butterfly Garden Two-way Shawl

The Butterfly Garden Square used for this shaped shawl is an original granny square used with permission from designer Chris Simon. Handpainted cotton yarn has subtle color variations that give the shawl a rich, organic look. I've designed this rectangular shawl with a bit of shaping by sewing shoulder seams and leaving armhole openings. In this configuration, the front edges drape naturally into bias folds, a popular look that can be casual or dressy.

YARN
Fine cotton, approximately 2,000 yd (1,840 m)

GAUGE
1 square = 6" x 6" (15 x 15 cm)

NOTIONS
Tapestry needle

FINISHED SIZE
18" x 72" (45.5 x 183 cm)

SHAPED SHAWL

Make 36 Butterfly Garden Squares (page 26). Arrange squares in a rectangle three squares wide by twelve squares long. Sew squares together with right sides facing, join from back loops of last row, following the diagram. Note that openings one and three-quarters squares deep are left four squares from each end for armholes. Join edge A to B and C to D to form shoulder seams.

PICOT EDGE

Work picots all around outside edges as follows: Join yarn in any corner st, *ch 3, sk 1 st, 1 sc in next st, rep from * all around, join with a Sl st in base of beg ch-3, fasten off.

Join yarn at underarm seam, work picot edge all around armhole opening. Repeat for other opening.

Blocking: Fold vest in half, place on a padded surface, spray with water, pat into shape with fingers, allow to dry.

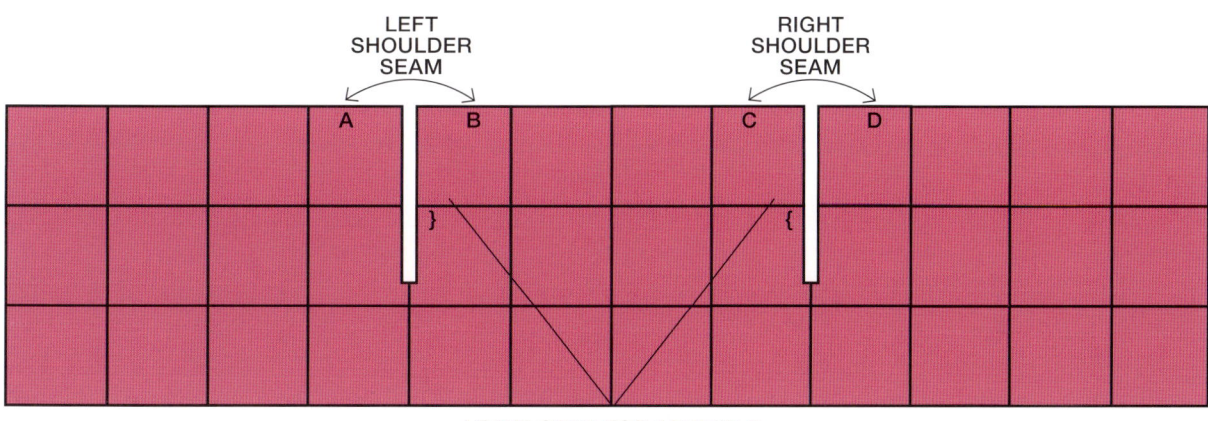

LEFT SHOULDER SEAM — A — B — RIGHT SHOULDER SEAM — C — D

LEAVE OPEN FOR ARMHOLE

RECTANGLE WRAP

To simplify the shawl, simply sew the squares together into a rectangle and add picot edging at the ends.

BUTTERFLY GARDEN SQUARE

Skill Level: Intermediate

Tr worked 3 rounds below: Yo (twice), insert hook in 4th dc of 7 skipped sts 3 rnds below, pick up a loop catching both ch-loops on both previous rnds, [yo, draw yarn through 2 loops on hook] 3 times.

Ch 4, join with a Sl st to form a ring.

Rnd 1: Ch 3 (counts as dc here and throughout), 15 dc in ring, join with a Sl st in 3rd ch of beg ch-3 (16 dc).

Rnd 2: Ch 3, (1 dc, ch 2, 2 dc) in same st (corner made), *1 dc in each of next 3 dc**, (2 dc, ch 2, 2 dc) in next dc (corner), rep from * twice, rep from * to ** once, join with a Sl st in 3rd ch of beg ch-3 (4 ch-2 corner sps).

Rnd 3: Sl st in next dc and in next ch-2 sp, ch 3, (1 dc, ch 2, 2 dc) in next ch-2 sp, *ch 6, sk next 7 dc, (2 dc, ch 2, 2 dc) in next corner ch-2 sp, rep from * twice, rep from * to ** once, join with a Sl st in 3rd ch of beg ch-3 (4 ch-6 sps, 4 ch-2 sps).

Rnd 4: Sl st in next dc and in next ch-2 sp, ch 3, (1 dc, ch 2, 2 dc) in same sp, *dc in next 2 dc, ch 6, sk next ch-6 sp, dc in each of next 2 dc**, (2 dc, ch 2, 2 dc) in next ch-2 sp, rep from * twice, rep from * to ** once, join with a Sl st in 3rd ch of beg ch-3 (4 ch-6 sps, 4 ch-2 sps).

Rnd 5: Sl st in next dc and in next ch-2 sp, ch 3, (1 dc, ch 2, 2 dc) in same sp, *1 dc in each of next 4 dc, ch 3, working over ch-loops in last 2 rnds, 1 tr in 4th dc of next 7 skipped dc in rnd 2, ch 3, 1 dc in each of next 4 dc**, (2 dc, ch 2, 2 dc) in next corner ch-2 sp, rep from * twice, rep from * to ** once, join with a Sl st in 3rd ch of beg ch-3 (8 ch-3 sps, 4 ch-2 sps).

Rnd 6: Sl st in next dc and in next ch-2 sp, ch 1, *(1 sc, ch 2, 1 sc) in same sp, 1 sc in each of next 6 dc, 3 sc in the next ch-3 sp, 1 sc in next tr, 3 sc in next ch-3 sp, 1 sc in each of next 6 dc, rep from * around, join with a Sl st in first sc.

Rnd 7: Sl st in next ch-2 sp, ch 3, (1 dc, ch 2, 2 dc) in same sp, *ch 6, sk next 7 sc, 1 dc in each of next 7 sc, ch 6, sk next 7 sc**, (2 dc, ch 2, 2 dc) in next corner ch-2 sp, rep from * twice, rep from * to ** once, join with a Sl st in 3rd ch of beg ch-3.

Rnd 8: Sl st in the next dc and in next ch-2 sp, ch 3, (1 dc, ch 2, 2 dc) in same sp, *1 dc in each of next 2 dc, ch 6, sk next ch-6 sp, 1 dc in each of next 7 dc, ch 6, sk next ch-6 sp, 1 dc in each of next 2 dc**, (2 dc, ch 2, 2 dc) in next corner ch-2 sp, rep from * twice, rep from * to ** once, join with a Sl st in 3rd ch of beg ch-3.

Rnd 9: Sl st in next dc and in next ch-2 sp, ch 3, (1 dc, ch 2, 2 dc) in same sp, *1 dc in each of next 4 dc, ch 3, working over ch-loops in last 2 rnds, 1 tr in 4th sc of next 7 skipped sc in rnd 6, ch 3, 1 dc in each of next 7 dc, ch 3, working over ch-loops in last 2 rnds, 1 tr in 4th sc of 7 skipped sc in rnd 6, ch 3, 1 dc in each of next 4 dc**, (2 dc, ch 2, 2 dc) in next corner ch-2 sp, rep from * twice, rep from * to ** once, join with a Sl st in 3rd ch of beg ch-3.

Rnd 10: Sl st in next dc and in next ch-2 sp, ch 1, *(1 sc, ch 2, 1 sc) in corner ch-2 sp, 1 sc in each of next 6 dc, 3 sc in next ch-3 sp, 1 sc in next tr, 3 sc in next ch-3 sp, 1 sc in each of next 7 dc, 3 sc in next ch-3 sp, 1 sc in next tr, 3 sc in next ch-3 sp, 1 sc in each of next 6 dc, rep from * around, join with a Sl st in first sc. Fasten off.

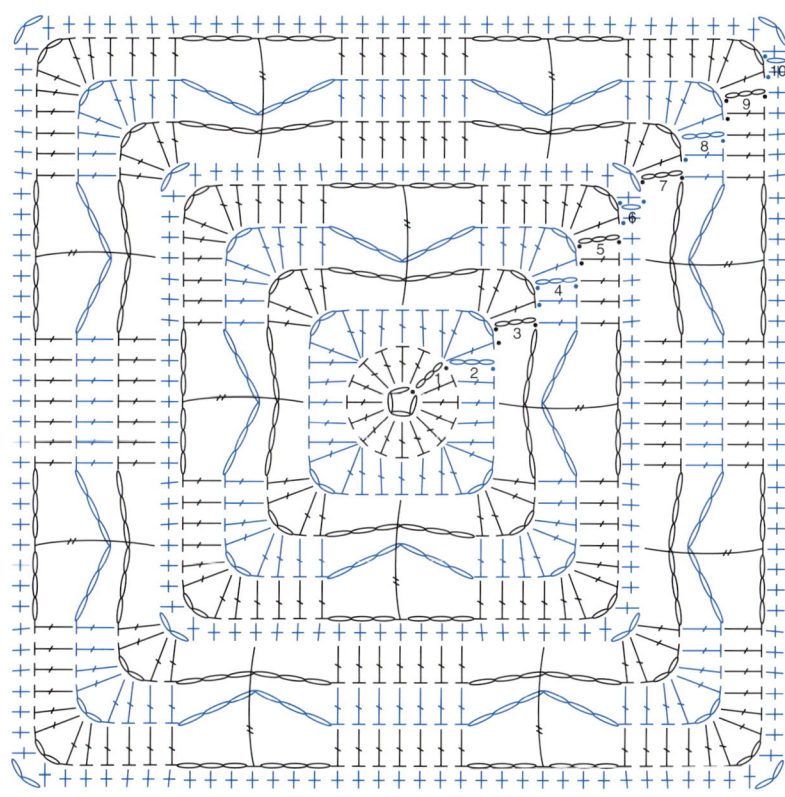

Popcorns and Lace Shawl

Granny square lace? Absolutely! This lovely cashmere and silk lace-weight yarn works up beautifully following the directions for the Popcorns and Lace Square. Finishing this shawl is a breeze, too, because you simply stitch the squares together in a long V shape. I added a scalloped edging to finish it off. Light as a feather and warm as a hug, this shawl is truly a dream to wear.

SHAWL

Make 20 Popcorns and Lace Squares (page 30).

Assemble the squares following the diagram, using a single crochet seam.

EDGING

Triple crochet 3 together (tr3tog): *Yo twice, pick up a loop in designated stitch, [yo, draw through 2 loops on hook] twice, rep from * twice in same stitch, yo, draw through all 4 loops on hook.

Work Three Petal Scallop on outside edges as follows:

Row 1: Working from RS, join yarn in bottom left corner ch-3 sp of scarf, * ch 8, Sl st in fourth ch from hook (picot made), ch 4, sk next 3 dc and 1 ch-1 sp, 1 sc in next ch-1 sp, ch 8, Sl st in fourth ch from hook (picot made), sk next 3 ch-1 sps, 1 sc in next dc, ch 8, Sl st in fourth ch from hook (picot made), ch 4, sk next 3 ch-1 sps, sc in next sp, ch 8, Sl st in fourth ch from

(continued)

YARN
Fine cashmere/silk, approximately 980 yd (910 m)

HOOK
6/G (4 mm)

GAUGE
1 square = 6" x 6" (15 x 15 cm)

NOTIONS
Tapestry needle

FINISHED SIZE
13" x 38" (33 x 96.5 cm)

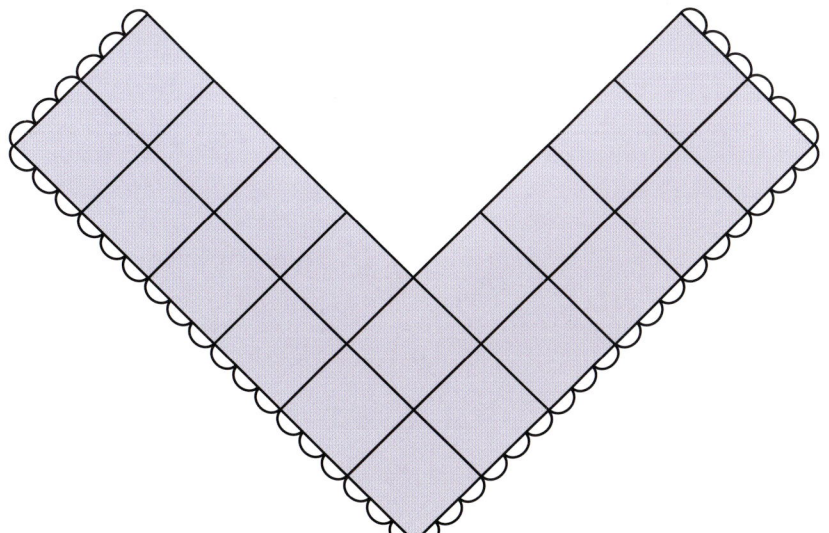

hook (picot made), ch 4, 1 sc in corner sp, 1 sc in corner sp of next square. Repeat from * around outer edge of shawl, turn.

Row 2: Ch 4, *[tr3tog, ch 5, tr3tog, ch 5, tr3tog] in next picot, 1 tr in next sc, rep from * around, ch 4, join with Sl st to beginning corner sp, fasten off.

If blocking is needed, lay on a padded surface, spray lightly with water, pat into shape, allow to dry.

POPCORNS AND LACE SQUARE

Beginning cluster (beg cluster): Ch 3, [yo (twice), insert hook in st or sp, yo, draw up a loop, yo, draw through 2 loops] 3 times in same st or sp, yo, draw through 4 loops on hook.

Cluster: [Yo (twice), insert hook in st or space, yo, draw up a loop, yo, draw through 2 lps] 4 times in same st or space, yo, draw through 5 loops on hook.

Beginning popcorn (beg pc): Ch 3 (counts as dc), 4 dc in same st or sp, drop loop from hook, insert hook in the 3rd ch of beg ch-3, pick up the dropped loop and draw through.

Popcorn (pc): Work 5 dc in same st or sp, drop loop from hook, insert hook in the first of the 5 dc just made, pick up dropped loop and draw through.

Ch 8, join with a Sl st to form a ring.

Rnd 1: Beg cluster in ring, *ch 3, 1 cluster in ring, ch 5**, 1 cluster in ring, rep from * twice, rep from * to ** once, join with a Sl st in 3rd ch of beg ch-3 (8 clusters, 4 ch-3 sps, 4 ch-5 sps).

Rnd 2: Sl st to center of next ch-3 sp, ch 1, 1 sc in same sp, *9 tr in the next ch-5 sp, 1 sc in next ch-3 sp, rep from * around, omit last sc, join with a Sl st in first sc (4 groups of 9 tr).

Rnd 3: Beg pc in first sc, *ch 2, sk next 2 tr, 1 dc in next tr, ch 2, sk next tr, (2 dc, ch 3, 2 dc) in next tr, ch 2, sk next tr, 1 dc in next tr, ch 2, sk next 2 tr**, 1 pc in next sc, rep from * twice, rep from * to ** once, join with a Sl st in top of first pc.

Rnd 4: Ch 3 (counts as dc), *[2 dc in ch-2 sp, 1 dc in next dc] twice, 1 dc in next dc, (2 dc, ch 3, 2 dc) in next ch-3 sp, 1 dc in next dc [1 dc in next dc, 2 dc in ch-2 sp] twice**, 1 dc in next pc, rep from * twice, rep from * to ** once, join with a Sl st in 3rd ch of beg ch-3.

Rnd 5: Ch 6 (counts as dc, ch 3), 1 dc in same st at base of ch-6, *sk next 2 dc, 1 dc in each of next 3 dc, 1 pc in next dc, 1 dc in each of next 3 dc, (2 dc, ch 3, 2 dc) in next ch-3 sp, 1 dc in each of next 3 dc, 1 pc in next dc, 1 dc in each of next 3 dc, sk next 2 dc**, (1 dc, ch 3, 1 dc) in next dc, rep from * twice, rep from * to ** once, join with a Sl st in 3rd ch of beg ch-6.

Rnd 6: Sl st to 2nd ch of next ch-3 sp, ch 4 (counts as dc, ch 1), *sk next dc, 1 dc in next dc, [ch 1, sk next st, 1 dc in next st] 4 times, (2 dc, ch 3, 2 dc) in next ch-3 sp, [1 dc in next dc, ch 1, sk next st] 5 times**, 1 dc in 2nd ch of next ch-3 sp, ch 1, rep from * twice, rep from * to ** once, join with a Sl st in 3rd ch of beg ch-4. Fasten off.

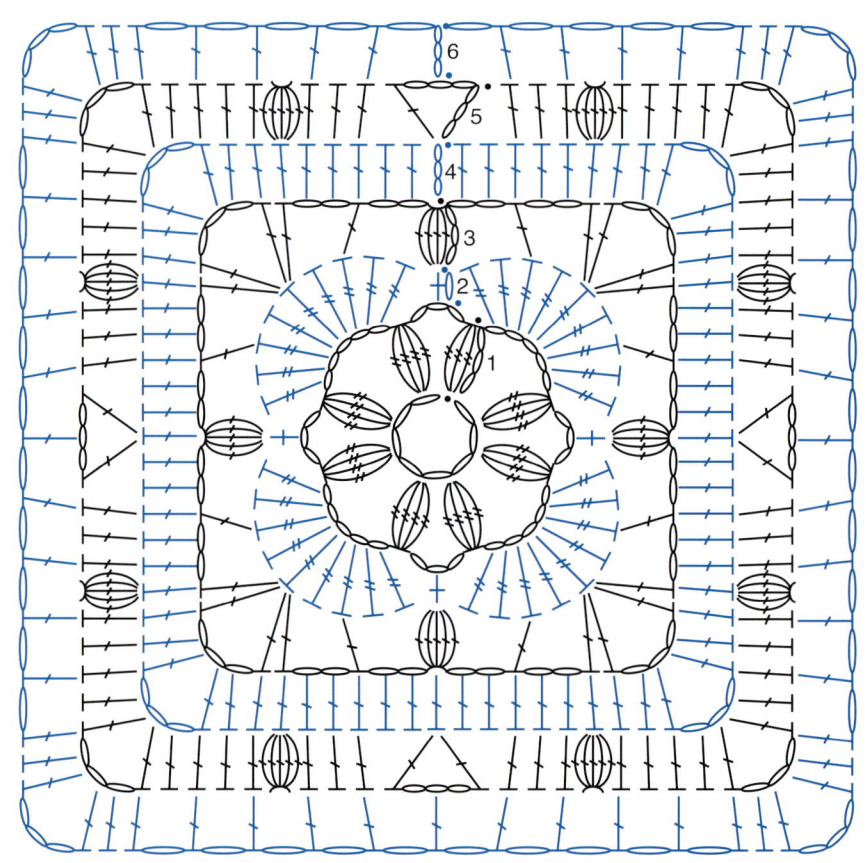

Abbreviations & Stitch Symbols

approx	approximately	FPdc	front post double crochet	sk	skip
beg	begin/beginning	FPsc	front post single crochet	Sl st	slip stitch
bet	between	FPtr	front post triple crochet	sp(s)	space(s)
BL	back loop(s)	g	gram(s)	st(s)	stitch(es)
bo	bobble	hdc	half double crochet	tbl	through back loop(s)
BPdc	back post double crochet	inc	increase/increases/increasing	tch	turning chain
BPsc	back post single crochet	lp(s	loop(s)	tfl	through front loop(s)
BPtr	back post triple crochet	Lsc	long single crochet	tog	together
CC	contrasting color	m	meter(s)	tr	triple crochet
ch	chain	MC	main color	trtr	triple triple crochet
ch-	refers to chain or space previously made e.g., ch-1 space	mm	millimeter(s)	tr2tog	triple crochet 2 together
ch lp	chain loop	oz	ounce(s)	TSS	Tunisian simple stitch
ch-sp	chain space	p	picot	WS	wrong side(s)
CL	cluster(s)	patt	pattern	yd	yard(s)
cm	centimeter(s)	pc	popcorn	yo	yarn over
cont	continue	pm	place marker	yoh	yarn over hook
dc	double crochet	prev	previous	[ ]	Work instructions within brackets as many times as directed
dc2tog	double crochet 2 stitches together	qutr	quadruple triple crochet	*	Repeat instructions following the single asterisk as directed
dec	decrease/decreases/decreasing	rem	remain/remaining	**	Repeat insructions between asterisks as many times as directed or repeated from a given set of instructions
dtr	double treble	rep	repeat(s)		
FL	front loop(s)	rev sc	reverse single crochet		
foll	follow/follows/following	rnd(s)	round(s)		
FP	front post	RS	right side(s)		
		sc	single crochet		
		sc2tog	single crochet 2 stitches together		

TERM CONVERSIONS

Crochet techniques are the same universally, and everyone uses the same terms. However, US patterns and UK patterns are different because the terms denote different stitches. Here is a conversion chart to explain the differences.

US	UK
single crochet (sc)	double crochet (dc)
half double crochet (hdc)	half treble (htr)
double crochet (dc)	treble (tr)
triple crochet (tr)	double treble (dtr)

CROCHET STITCH SYMBOLS

- ⬯ = chain
- • = slip st (sl st)
- + = single crochet
- = half double crochet (hdc)
- = double crochet (dc)
- = treble crochet (tr)
- = double treble crochet (dtr)
- = reverse sc
- = long sc
- = long dc
- = bullion st
- ⌢ = worked in back loop only
- ⌣ = worked in front loop only
- = picot
- = placement of st

- = front post dc (FPdc)
- = back post dc (BPdc)
- = front post trc (FPtrc)
- = sc3tog
- = dc2tog
- = dc3tog
- = bobbles
- = dc5tog
- = dc7tog
- = tr2tog
- = tr3tog
- = dtr2tog